MOSTLY LOVE

&

WORDS FOR

THOUGHT

JoAnne Lipari Evangelista

MOSTLY LOVE

&

WORDS FOR

THOUGHT

JoAnne Lipari Evangelista

JoAnne Lipari Evangelista Publishing
2015

MOSTLY LOVE & WORDS FOR THOUGHT
Copyright © 2015 by JoAnne Lipari Evangelista

First Printing: 2015

ISBN: 978-0-692-50558-8

JoAnne Lipari Evangelista Publishing
47625 Manorwood Drive
Northville, Michigan 48168

DEDICATION

I wish to dedicate this book not only to those who inspired and encouraged me to write, but also to the "art of poetry" itself. The writing of poetry helped me through some difficult emotional times and assisted me in growing both mentally and emotionally.

I want to especially dedicate this book to my parents, Louis and Lucy Lipari, for all of their love and support as I was growing up. I also want to dedicate this book to my husband, James, who encouraged me to pursue publishing my poetry.

JoAnne Lipari Evangelista

RHYMES

Timeless destiny reappears,
Peeking in from rainbow's end,
Turning round to find the villain,
Back again to find his friend.
Tapestry around the window,
Leaning out to no man's land,
Sing aloud in search of someone,
Bring it home to hide in sand.
Faraway the trumpet's sounding,
Echoes past the barnyard door,
Saying I won't find another,
Back to find the lion's roar.
People hide in zoom-in lenses,
Friends appear in tape and lime,
Apartment buildings tearing down,
Circles round the edge of time.
War begins to solve their problems,
Nameless faces stained in red,
Printing distorts time and person,
Bring around the thoughtless said.
Time corrupts the load and master,
Disappears into high tide,
Into dust flee mice and rabbits,
Round again the tables glide.
Notebooks hidden in small places,
Say "I love you", think it's true,
Round the corner come the bookends,
Back again it's only you.
Round my face the flowers growing,
Heads behind the New York Times,
Put back space with mere reminders,
With words together making rhymes.

BECAUSE

And I loved the cold
And I loved the storm
And I loved the challenge
And I loved the struggle
I even loved the pain,
Because I loved!

CRYING CRYSTAL TEARS

Crying crystal tears that float gently to the ground,
Laughing out of tune, yet, not making any sound.
Leaving not a footprint on the sand upon a beach,
Stalling for tomorrow, though it's always out of reach.
Pulling down the sky for stars and sea to meet,
Walking towards your goal by crawling on your feet.
Understanding love and yet losing all you care for,
Night has turned to light and the day is black, so therefore,

The 14-carat, gold-plated sunshine isn't spilling over a tarnished world.

A CHILD'S MAGIC WRITING BOARD

Erase you from my memory?
I cannot.
Your impression's there forever.

TOO LATE

I live in dreams; my goals are high;
The world seems perfect as a result.
But, like a balloon breaks, my dreams will too,
My goals, like a faded sun.
Then, when realization hits me,
I'll enter the world of reality.
I'll find it the opposite of my world.
I'll find it full of violence, full of hate.
I'll try to step back to my other world,
Where it's peaceful and calm,
But, I won't be able to,
For, like a broken balloon, it will not return,
But, eventually, what does?

SILENCE

Silence doesn't have to mean there are no words to be spoken.
Silence may be merely a time for words longing to be.

RAIN

As the rain comes falling down
And the sky, the lightning lights,
As the thunder shakes the house
Like many other stormy nights,
 I lie awake and think of you,
You, so very far away,
Counting the hours till you're back again,
And you're home to stay.

Outside the rain will soon have to stop,
The thunder and lightning as well,
And everything will be quiet again
Like it is when darkness has fell,
And I'll eventually fall asleep,
My thoughts of you for a while will be still,
But there will be rain falling oh so hard,
In my heart and it always will.

PARADOX

So you made me cry,
Should I hate you?
I cried because I missed the laughter,
The laughter and the happiness you made happen.
I guess I had to cry,
Because you made a beautiful thing end;
But, then again, you made that beautiful thing begin.

SWEET MEMORIES

Time goes by and I'm alone,
As I think, my thoughts do roam,
Raindrops fall as if they know of my sweet memories.

Since you've gone, I cry each day,
Wondering what took you away,
All I'm left with is to say,
I still love you so.

Remembering all the fun we had
Only makes me feel so blue.
To reminisce of the love we shared
Only adds to my love for you.

And so I'll live each passing year,
Thinking of our love so dear,
Until the day when I'll be near,
To share our memories,
Sweet memories.

WAS IT? IS IT?

Was it you I really loved?
> OR

Was it love?

How can I ask either question, when the word really didn't exist.
I fooled myself then, before,
> NOW?

REFLECTION

Are you real or are you fake?
If I touch you, will you break?
Is your laugh just for show?
So no one knows you're hurting so?
Do you ever shed a tear?
Let someone know you think they're dear?
Were you ever hurt inside?
So hurt that you broke down and cried?
When will you learn to act naturally?
Oh mirror, please, won't you answer me?

LISTEN

I never said I didn't care.
I just said I didn't love you.

MEMORIES

Memories are objects
More precious to us than gold,
They can't be seen or touched
And they're impossible to hold.
They bring about our happiness
Of the years gone by,
They remind us of our past
And of how the time does fly.
They reminisce the good times,
Trying to forget the bad,
When reminded of our happy times,
We can't forget the sad.
Yet, we seem to love them all
Although some bring us pain,
For we know that at no time
Will they come to life again.

GAME OF LIFE; PART I

I knew the object of the game.
All the money was there and the game board;
But, where are the men?

ODE TO LOVE

Love, love, you were so young,
But you did come to me.
I was so glad to see you come,
I had dreamed how it would be.

You made my days pass easily,
For I thought that you would grow.
You started oh so very young,
But I knew I loved you so.

Then the disappointment came,
And all I did was cry.
For I found out you would never grow,
You had already begun to die.

The pain of each new passing day
Pierced and stung my heart,
For together we had never been
And already we were to part.

Why oh why did you ever come,
For you tore my heart in two.
Cause I loved you, yes, I really did,
And, yet, he never knew.

GAME OF LIFE; PART II

Why is it that
When the game is over
Do I suddenly remember the rules?

AUTUMN COMING

The sky was so dark
Shining were each star,
The night was so clear
You could see from afar.

Quiet was the night
And by standing in the breeze,
You could hear the gentle whisper
Between the wind and the nearby trees.

Softly came the whispers
But, if you listened, you could hear
That summer was soon ending
And fall would soon be near.

Quietly they ended
And spoke their final word,
And if you stayed a moment longer
Not a sound you could have heard.

ADULT GAMES

We play childish games of hiding and searching,
Hiding who we are and expecting others to find us,
But others may not have the time
And not the desire, some,
And so they move on to those of us
Playing childish games of showing and telling.

AUTOBIOGRAPHY

Opportunity knocks but once
But I'm afraid to open the door.
I feel I've got time
And when my fear is gone,
I'll let Opportunity in.

I hesitate, as if the door were stuck.
Finally, I make up my mind.
Slowly, but steadily, I open the door to
     No one.
Then I cry and walk outside.
I call and call to
     No one.

Is he deaf?
Does he not see?
Opportunity's gone.
Oh wait – There he is, but he's knocking elsewhere
And the door has opened....
Gone.

ARTICLE CHANGE

How different
When "a" becomes "the."

UNKNOWN LOVE

There are so many things I wish I could say
Each time I see you pass my way.
But, I get all shaky and nervous inside,
And all my feelings I have to hide.
I try to speak, but the words won't come,
My hands perspire; my knees feel numb.
By the time I'm calm, you've gone away,
And I have to wait for still another day.

MEANING

I was recently told
That loss of Meaning
Is serious.
I guess it's been a serious thing
Since I lost you.

SMALL BOY

Small boy running, falling, laughing,
Unaware of what's around
Knowing only of love and laughter,
Only caring about play and fun
Marveling at the world around us.

Small boy yelling, spelling, reading,
Off to school he goes
Trying hard to keep his grades up,
Brings an apple for the teacher
Thinking girls are just for hitting.

Small boy driving, smoking, drinking,
Beginning to know what life's about
Falling in love for probably the first time,
Trying hard to maintain an image
Feels depressed but keeps his head up.

Small boy running, falling, shooting,
Striving hard for his survival
Knowing only of death and hatred,
Only choice to kill or be killed
The ugliness of the world we're part of.

Small boy dead before his time
Why?

SIMPLICITY

Why is it so Difficult to
Attain that which would make all else so simple?
Perhaps the Difficulty lies in its Simplicity.

CHANCE

Sirens blow
And, yet, you know
There's time for you to stay,
For once you're gone, you won't return.
Raindrops fall
And, still, you call
My name out in the crowd,
But, I will no longer answer.

    Free, I'm free,
    No ties have I to bind my expansive mind.
    Gone, I've gone to find myself among the ruins of our time.

Sad eyes cry
And, so do I,
The light has turned to dark.

I GUESS

I guess I spend too much time
Chasing rainbows that aren't,
Smashing into roadblocks that are.

HARVEST

Now I realize
You didn't have to speak,
My answer was there in your silence.
Still, I waited,
Waited patiently,
No answer.
Confusion sought my mind,
Illusion was dissolved,
Fragments pierced my heart as they fell.
Still I waited,
No answer.
Now my resolution's here,
Sad, the way things turn out,
That look – wasn't it?
That silence – was it!
Funny, what a fool one could be.
Buffy, I'll be that farmer!

TENDENCY

I've a tendency to love,
Watch me.
I've a tendency to be hurt,
Same difference.

MISTAKEN

I thought and thought and analyzed,
I planned,
I read into your eyes
And listened to your smiles,
And I was mistaken.
Mistaken like before
But worse,
This time was real.
You were different.
The others were fakes.
You were real all right,
And I,
I was mistaken.

A PIECE ON TIME OR A TIMEPIECE

Round and round,
End where begun
   And, yet,
Progressing?

MY HEART

You touched my heart with your eyes,
It sang!

My eyes beheld a vision circling around me,
Enclosing me in a cloud of dreams.
I awoke in a serene meadow,
Listening to the trees whisper.
Fade....

The meadow faded into blue.
I was encircled by blue.
Dark....

A candle was glowing or was it the eye of a tiger?
My heart was crying.

A LOVE POEM

I've wanted to write a love poem,
Yet it seems I can't find the right words.
Perhaps it's because Love is hard to define,
Love is that which needs no words,
Love IS.

DISSOLVE

Your laugh was warm,
Your touch was soft,
You calmed my senses,
I needed that.

You told me a secret,
I promised not to tell,
You smiled as if knowing,
I needed that.

You kissed my lips,
It kissed my heart,
All was right,
I needed that.

I ran outside,
You followed laughing,
You caught my arm,
I needed that.

We fell together,
I kissed your face,
You caressed my body,
I needed that.

The sun grew cold,
You said good-bye,
Your hand touched mine,
I needed that.

Your smile has waned,
Your touch is gone. Your love is cold....

24 HOURS

Looking back over the green fields of Yesterday,
I found myself yearning for the gate
To bear a sign "Open 24 hours".

IF NOW WAS THEN

If now was then
How strange!
Passing glances, friendly
Passing strangers, neighbors.

If now was then
I could have followed
And round about
Our paths would have crossed necessarily
As they will now.

How strange is life!
How I once longed to be a part of your landing
And now I might be
But the magic's gone.
It's now a dream once dreamt.
It's only a good memory.

If now was then
If....
If is such a meaningless word!

RUNNING AWAY

For the first time I told myself,
If the relationship grew to a solid commitment,
I would not run.

You ran……………

SELF-ADVICE

The spinning must end!
Gone are the souvenirs. Do not discard them, but hide them well.
Dreams exist.
Do not destroy the seed.
It will blossom with enough care and want.
Oh, it will wilt, but that's no reason to destroy the seed.
Reality's there;
Do not stamp it out, as it will not leave so easily.
It will push the door down as it has in the past.
Fantasy can last only so long,
Then it too must die.
Do not mistake it for Creativity.
You're alive – LIVE!
Let your soul be naked to the sun.
Raise your arms and run laughing through the woods.
Speak the word and let the flow come rushing.
Do not dam it, as that would be fake.
Dig up that treasure and share it,
Share it with all, not just a select few.
Darkness exists,
If only to show light;
Turn off the switch and you will see.
Why?
Because you have stopped searching
For that which cannot be found.
You gave up your search as hopeless.
You resigned yourself to believing
It is non-existent.
I Am.
You Are.

ACCEPTANCE

Can I accept the Whole without accepting all of its Parts?

A PLEA

Why is it so easy to be difficult?
I could smile now
I could laugh now
But I cry now.
The value is realized
But, is it too late?
Why does realization come too often too late?
Happiness is splintered in all directions,
Each sliver more piercing than the previous.
I try to maintain stability but
Even rocks fall and crack.
Please, please
Let there be a second chance,
Please.
The dream is slipping,
Slowly, slowly it is melting away.
There's time to preserve it,
The wound can be sealed,
There's time,
But is there a chance?
Please.

SOMEONE

If to you I am someone,
Then my being is of worth.

I AM

I'm real!
Believe me
I feel,
I'm not stone.
Although I hide my feelings,
They Are.
Feelings exist in me
And I hurt,
Man, do I hurt
And I cry.
Yes, I cry real tears.
I may not cry out
But inside I'm screaming.

I'm real!
Touch me
I'm warm
And my limbs move,
Not like a robot,
Like a human
I talk too,
And I see and hear and smell and taste.
But most important, I feel.
I see the sunrise
And I feel its warmth.
I hear Russell
And I feel his soul.
I smell autumn
And I feel its chill.
I taste the wine
And I feel its strength.
I feel! I feel! I FEEL!!

FRIENDS

You and me,
We.

Hand in hand,
Together.

Sharing a tear,
Borrowing a smile,
Lending a thought,
FRIENDS.

DREAM OF REALITY

I had been lonely,
Not alone but lonely,
Then you came.
You were lonely too,
I sensed it.
But, I wanted you to realize
It takes two halves to make one whole,
Two whole halves to make one whole,
Separate them,
They're still whole.
Adjoin them,
They're a larger whole.
I was alone,
Then you came,
I grew,
You grew,
Together.

A MOVIE

We watched them
And I almost spoke their lines.

How was I to know what caused them to part
Would be the opposite of ours.

FAREWELL TO SAVANNAH

Good-bye,
I didn't say it yesterday,
I didn't want to.
Once before you walked out of my life,
But this time was different,
I really knew you.

You, you have so much to give and you do,
But, realize it!
Do not down you
And don't let others influence.

That look,
I've come across it before.
There's much more below the surface and I think you know.
I wish I could have confirmed it,
I didn't,
I could only go on guessing.

If only our roles were switched,
I think you would have learned.
I wanted so much to blurt out the lesson.
Instead, I made lesson plans to be discarded with the course.
I only wish you had realized and asked.
Now, there's only one link left,
Solder it and let it last forever.

Good-bye.
I didn't say it yesterday
But I must, today.
I wanted so to take that longing look away,
I only hope she does.

TALKING

I thought it was that
We needed to talk,
But we've done enough talking
And now need to communicate.

YOU ARE GONE

I tried desperately to hold on.
I stretched out my arm and frantically reached.
I was able to touch you.
Yes, it was you.
I touched you!

But… but…
But my grip wasn't strong enough.
The wind carried you away.
You were suddenly gone and I was alone.

Oh, but you need not come back.
My grip isn't any stronger
And I couldn't stand the pain.
I only want to know,
Why did you leave me holding?
Why did you float away without warning?
You left me here with only a memory
And, for yourself, you took a part never to be replaced.

I closed my eyes,
Hoping that when I reopened my eyes,
My extended hand would be filled.

I opened my eyes…

A FAIRYE TALE

I seem to not know when it's over.
Without happily-ever-after,
I get confused.

LOOK AT ME!

Look at me!
It's been so long
I hope you still remember me.
No, you haven't changed,
It's me who's changed.
I no longer fantasize,
No longer dream,
My needs are greater,
I've matured.

Look at me!
Can you see the difference?
Do you know how I've felt, this year, without you?
No, you don't know,
But I do.
Empty.
No longer can I believe you're there,
No longer do I reminisce.

Look at me!
I've changed.
I'm no longer the same.
A part of me is gone,
You.

TO TOUCH

I think it's just the wind touching the night leaves,
To remind us that to touch is to be.

WE

"We" were so close, too close, for too short a time.
All was right and "we" knew it.
Then it came,
The End.
"We" tried to postpone it,
It won.
Now here "I" am,
"We" is now "I"
And how lonely and unhappy "I" can be.

WHY?

Why is it when we love we can't,
And when we don't, we can?

ME

ME was so hidden for so long
Within characters and plots and scenes.
ME finally emerged center stage and went unrecognized,
As if the characters and plots and scenes had been me.
But, ME was playing the part,
And ME was oh so tired.
Thank you for bringing ME to me.

HONESTY

You claimed it was one of the all-important desirables,
And I agreed again and again.
Yet, when we parted and I alone stopped to think,
I realized it had been missing.

CHOICE

I must choose
And that's what makes me sad.
I think of you and you and you
And know we all cannot be.
Yet, you each served a purpose,
Each of you meant something
And some of you meant more.
For that I am thankful,
Thankful that each of you happened;
I'm thankful that our paths one day crossed.
You were each an inn along the roadside
Where I stopped to rest for varying times.
You each shared my dreams, my thoughts and my smiles,
And some of you shared my tears.
Then I journeyed on,
Many times not wanting to,
But many times having to.
For a traveller can only be at one place at one time
And whenever I thought I found HOME,
It was time to travel on.

I must choose
Yes, one day I must choose
And that's what makes me sad,
For the rest of you will not be a part of WE.
Yet there is a ray of brightness,
For You and You and You and I
Will always share a part of that road.
You and You and You and I
Were once WE.
For that I am Thankful.

FOR

I'm sorry
For what was and can no longer be,
For what wasn't and now is,
For me
And for you,
And for us
Not surviving.

THE LEAVES ARE NICE

"The leaves are nice,
You can come now."
And so my journey begins.
I am Free!
Free from the hassles and the farce,
Free from the games,
Free with him and Nature.
There's so much there,
So much he has taught me.

One doesn't need a manual to confirm existence.
Open your heart, not a book,
And you'll learn.
I have.
It may have taken a long time,
But I've learned.
Please understand,
It's not you I despise,
It's what you represent.
You make me be the person I'm longing to escape.
Please understand,
He is good for me.
I want you to realize
I'm not doing this to hurt you.
I love you too,
But the leaves are nice
And I must go.

MONOCHROMATIC MONDAY

One color, one day,
    Blue.
As in sky, as in water,
    And ME.

HOW UGLY

I thought you were different.
I really believed you weren't like the others,
That you did care,
But, now I'm disillusioned.
Not because I feel I've lost you,
But that I've lost faith,
Faith in someone I thought so beautiful,
Someone who originally restored my faith in the others,
After I believed them all to be fakes.
Now I feel my original beliefs were right.
My one beautiful person isn't all that beautiful,
How ugly!

GAMES

We were playing games by rules you made up.

How were you to know your custom-made rules were the reason
you'd lose it all?

LOOKING

Looking at you saddens me.
I see myself reflected in your glasslike eyes
And I wonder,
Wonder if ever the glass does shatter,
Will I shatter too?
Or will I be there to piece the splinters together
And draw the drapes for the night.

ODE TO A TELEPHONE

I
Waited
And waited
For you to tell me
He still cared.
Why did you remain Silent?

ONE WORLD

Why can't I tell you the truth?
It's so beautiful and so pure,
Yet you would think differently.
You would get angry and call me a fool.
But I was happy,
We were stardust and you can't change that.
Don't try to make the two worlds so divided,
They will become one if you allow it.
If you come between us,
We just might lose.
The choice is yours, not mine.
We can both be a part of the same world,
          Our world.

THE WINNING

I may lose,
Yes, I may lose,
But in order to ever win,
I must play the game.

MASSACHUSSETS

It was the longest day,
Yet the shortest weekend,
As the golden curtain fell and rose again,
And our gentle laughter floated.
I felt the rush within me surge
As my eyes melted with your eyes,
And I still wonder who was I when I was with you.

NO TRESPASSING

The grass always looks greener,
And, man, did I see green.
But what I didn't see,
Was "Private Property".

THE MOMENT

We smashed the fallen leaves as we walked along in step,
And I raised my eyes to watch the autumn breeze dancing with
    your hair.
Around us, blurs of faces; some of friends and some unknown,
Yet all were lost in the serenity of the moment.
Our steps began to quicken as the blurs began to fade,
And my ears picked up the sounds they hadn't heard before.
The leaves no longer silently fell beneath my feet,
And the space beside me was vacant.

TO A YOUNG POETESS

Deeply touched,
I felt the trickle of warmth caressing the flesh of my cheek.
My sensitive little friend, thank you!

PROPHET

You're special you are
With your golden hair flowing and your smile,
Your smile could melt any frown.
I watch you as you bring the rest together,
Never leaving anyone behind.
When you speak, your words flow honestly.
You simply move my inner soul.
I long to reach out and touch you,
But I'm afraid,
Afraid that if I do, you'll fade
And like crystal droplets, vanish.
Yet, I remain here,
Hoping your prophecy will include me.
I long to share it,
Though my feelings won't change even if
Your eyes tell me no.

ETERNAL QUESTION

There will be one you won't forget
Though fate has passed you by,
And always when he comes to mind
You'll ask, well what if I?

ODE TO A HOUSE

Tonight's the last night I'll be with you.
I'll miss you.
Your walls hold many a secret
You'll never get a chance to reveal.
For you possess ten years of memories,
All somehow loved and for some reason relived.
Now you'll become another's,
Recording a new history,
But don't forget me,
We shared a lot, you and I.

I'M SORRY

Rivers overflowing the banks of My Eyes;
What more can I say?

My WORLD

For the first time in My Life
I thought I found something,
Something real in a world of fantasy,
But you vanished
And left me with a real and empty world.

CRY OF HELP

Can one not see an extended hand is not usually left unfilled?
I guess too many Ones
Are simply blinded by Self,
Paralyzing the hand from reaching.

I BELIEVED

I really believed we had a beautiful thing going.

I really believed you cared for me in a way no one's cared for me before.

I really believed I finally found someone who knew the real me and liked me.

I really believed I was falling in love with you.

I really believed I found the man I dreamed of but gave up hope of finding.

If only you had believed too.

YOURSELF

Everyone's looking, but what do they find?
Everyone's looked, but nobody's found.
I've been looking and it's a drag.
It seems I can't even find myself.

MY PLAY

It was a perfect ending,
As I silently walked away
And with a loving look in your eyes,
You watched me.
All the pieces seemed to fit,
Yet now I finally realize
Our love could've been set to music on a stage.

But this, this is different.
You are real, as real as I
And I no longer have to act,
Yet I do.
I guess I've thought it was the same,
Just another plot, another play,
But, there's no stage,
No music,
Only you.

ONE

Too many times I've called for a recount,
And I still end up with one.

WE'RE TOGETHER

We're together.
It's summer
And we're laughing in the sun,
And riding through the mountains,
Never thinking of tomorrow,
Yet, it comes.
We say good-bye,
Somehow feeling it isn't,
And it's not.

We're together.
It's autumn
And you and me, we talk,
We both become more knowing,
Never worrying about the future,
But, it's there.
We say good-bye,
Somehow feeling it isn't,
And it's not.

We're together.
It's winter
And our relationship is strained.
I seem to want commitment,
Cause I'm thinking of tomorrow,
Which will come.
We say good-bye,
Is it?

KNOWING ME

In order to know me,
I must step outside me
And see me as others see me.
Only then, could I love you.

GOLDEN PEOPLE

As November fades, I think back to autumn,
To October and to us, the golden people,
To our dreams of Maine, and our reality of Mass,
To my unmatched feeling of joy and contentment,
Contentment of being with three people I loved.
As November fades, I think back to autumn,
To October and to us, the golden people,
To you three, I am thankful,
Thankful for an October I'll always remember.

PROTECTION

I built up a wall
So I'd be unharmed,
But then the wall I built up
Kept me from you.

HAPPY BIRTHDAY

I spoke to you today,
But somehow I feel it wasn't enough.
I wanted so to tell you I miss you.
I wanted so to say,
Please hurry down here.
I wanted so to ask if you missed me.
I wanted so to tell you
I'm always thinking of you.

I did say Happy Birthday,
But somehow I feel it wasn't enough.

ME'S TO BLAME

Why do I keep hidden that which I want all to see?
Maybe cause once it's shown,
What could I then blame for your leaving?

A SUPERSTAR

I watched you,
As you followed the script,
Saying the words needed to be spoken.
Each part fell into place,
For nothing was left out,
And a chill swept through me as it ended.
You made it, and I was happy
As I watched you beam in the applause.
I walked out,
Feeling deeply affected,
And I just couldn't leave you.
I was impressed,
Impressed by your splendor,
So I waited.
Soon you appeared,
And somehow the splendor was gone.
You were young.
Was I older than you?
You smiled.
I smiled.
You walked away, alone.
I watched you
As you disappeared into the crowd,
But every so often you glanced back.
Were you looking for me?
Somehow the splendor was gone.
You were lonely.
Was I happier than you?
A tear fell
For you,
For all the others,
How ironic: Superstar!

PERPLEXED

Why does love give me pain?
OR
Does my pain bring me love?

I WONDER

Are you thinking now?
I know your time has changed,
And I wonder.
Did you receive my message?
I know it should be there,
And I wonder.
I wonder if I'll ever hear your voice again
Or just hear its echo in my mind.
I miss your voice.
I miss you.
Are you missing me now?
Are you thinking of me now?
Tomorrow your fair weather friends will be gone.
And where will you be?
Don't give up!
Are you thinking now?
Where will you be? What will you have?
There are real people,
Turn around.
Will you see me?
And I wonder.

I'M ALONE

Why does it seem
Whenever I stop to think,
I'm alone?

ONCE AGAIN

The glances spoke of windless seas and windmill dreams,
As I wallowed through those that were and those that weren't,
Escaping.
I wanted so to have it all,
Not realizing, all was already mine.
Silently longing, I awakened to dreams
Transforming into roadblocks of Time.
Heedlessly leaping,
I felt unsure of the glances I once knew were mine,
And I was scared once again.

ON GROWING UP

Can't you see it's fading?
The blue's becoming gray,
As the sun melts to the ground,
Smearing the sky with a warm red glow.
But, you're pretending not to see,
Pretending it's not come,
Holding onto yesterday,
       Today.

THE WINNER

Tears silently cascading
To a softened pool of gloom,
Not knowing it was Silence
That made them flow.
Longing to cry out "Why",
I sit and stare
At you on the paper before me,
Knowing if it weren't for the Silence,
You would not exist.
You are the creation,
Which I gave birth to,
Thereby making me the winner.
For although I lost him,
I did have him,
And you, you I shall have forever.
Poor fool that he was,
All he had was part of me!

REMEMBRANCE

Why must my mind remember what your heart forgot?

SAD BOY

Sad boy sitting, staring at a cement wall separating him from me;
Will the music of the night change the tempo of his time?
Or, will he be there, tomorrow, gazing at the freedom
That's only a mere reflection of his mind.

WORDS OF YOU

As long as you appear in words,
I find you never to be gone.

HERE and THERE

I really cared
And somehow still do,
And yet you,
You've been noncommittal.
But, he's come
And I care,
But in a different way;
You're there
And he's here,
And I need someone
Here and now.

In summer you told me,
If only I were there.
Now it's spring
And I'm telling you,
If only you were here.
But, you're not,
As I wasn't,
And I guess that's why it's goodbye.

TODAY'S TOMORROW'S YESTERDAY

Yesterday,
Rain distorted my perception.
Today,
Sun is blinding the truth.
Tomorrow…

ADVICE

We've discussed it often,
Along with its qualifications,
And we decided what was wrong and what was right.
But here I sit,
Pen in hand, tear in eye,
And realize we've been wrong!
What matters most is what you have,
And my advice is
Hold On!
We saw in others,
Maybe what we envied,
Maybe what we admired,
Maybe what we wanted,
But was it what we needed?

How much longer can we endure silence?
How much longer can we endure games?
How much longer can we endure pain?
How much longer can we endure?
The missing link we've been searching for
May have been overlooked by our blindness.
Maybe it's that which cannot be attained
And maybe we thought we saw it in others,
But we could have been wrong.
Hold on, I repeat, hold on!
I only hope I am able to find what you've got,
And I hope I'll know enough to hold on.
For one needs substance to hold on to.
Dreams, they slip away,
And then one's left,
Pen in hand, tear in eye,
Realizing one's been so wrong!

WHO I AM

Why must I be what I'm not in order to be who I am?

A SONG FOR ALLISON

Brown long hair flowing,
Along in a metaphorical tone,
Oh so gentle,
Yet, I can sometimes sense a tempest brewing.
Is loneliness the cause of the white walls so often referred to?
Or is Pierre penning the letter you spent nights composing?
I often wonder,
Wonder why a good person such as yourself,
Should seem so alone,
And I wonder more about what's hidden
Behind those rose-colored glasses,
Than what's visibly in front of them.

CYCLES

Greenery silently waving its untouched hands across my foot
To caress the ever-changing of its magical carpet,
While I sit complaining about all that's the same.

A CHANGE IN TIME

What a change has come over me!
I shall soon see you
And once again enter your world,
A world that at one time meant more to me than my own,
A world that at one time was my entire life.

What a change has come over me!
I now see you as you really are,
A part of a world so different from mine,
A part of a world to become part of
I'd have to sacrifice me.

What a change has come over me!
I may soon see you,
But now I mean I don't care,
When I say it.

What a change has come over me!
Although I did need you,
I needed you to give me the confidence
To stand in my world,
To show me I belonged in my world.

I now feel as I felt the first time I was to meet you.
I will because I promised.
I no longer yearn to see you and why?
Because now I'll see you the way you really are,
And I'm afraid the magic of those five months will fade.
I no longer care,
And in some way I wish I still did,
But the magic's gone and reality's come,
And, man, what a change has come over me!

LOVE MEDITATION

Don't ask me to love everyone,
For then I couldn't possibly love you.

IT'S ALL CHANGED NOW

We parted friends,
And yet I sense,
Our friendship is of no worth.
Friends we cannot be,
You know as well as I,
For always will the past remind us, remind us of what was.

It's all changed now!
You realize as well as I,
Although we've asked what happened,
Our question remains unanswered.

Friends we parted,
And yet I sense,
Friends we cannot be,
For feelings had surpassed friends,
And how can we turn back?

We can only move ahead,
Or begin where we detoured,
But to friends we cannot go,
For there we had not been.

ON WRITING

I find not much to write these days.
Is it that I've run out of words?
        OR
Is it that my pen has no ink?
        NO!
I guess I too often spend my time,
Juggling the words in my mind,
And deciding they're just not worth a rhyme!

STOP CRYING!

Stop crying!
No need to carry on.
It's over and nothing you do will change that.

Stop crying!
Pull yourself together.
Life goes on,
And new love will unfold.

Stop crying!
No one will kiss a tear-stained cheek.
And besides,
In order to gain love, one must give,
Not a tear, but a smile.

Stop crying!
It's not for him you weep.
You feel sorry for you.
But that's life,
And he was a good but finite part of your life.

Stop crying!
Why be sad?
Let the past be past,
But also let it be a lesson,
For life is a continuum
Of yesterdays, todays and tomorrows,
None of which can be isolated.
Stop crying!
And open your eyes.
You may do something you never did before,
SEE!

EYES

The world we once knew has almost dissolved.
What could have been no longer even exists.
But, time and again,
Our eyes will meet,
And what will they be saying?

SOMETIMES

Sometimes it's a terrible thing to be right,
    Sometimes.
Sometimes it's a painful thing to be right,
    Sometimes.
Sometimes I feel it's a terrible thing to be,
    Sometimes.
Sometimes I feel it's a painful thing to be,
    Sometimes.
Sometimes it seems so useless,
    Sometimes.
Sometimes it seems worthwhile,
    Sometimes.
Sometimes I know not how I feel,
    Sometimes.
        NOW?

LOVE IS...

Love's dust upon my palm
Awaiting a strong breeze to
Whisk it off to you.

A SIMILAR DISTORTION

Rain, you're distorting on my window,
As I speed along the thruway,
As you had once before,
When I was travelling another highway.
But, it was autumn, not early summer,
And I was smiling, not battling tears,
And someone was beside me,
And that made all the difference.

GRAMMAR

I found the object,
Now I only need the verb.

YESTERDAY'S NO LONGER

Tomorrow I may not love you
As I had yesterday,
When our hearts were intertwined.
Tomorrow I may not touch you
As yesterday I did,
When we both stood as one.
Tomorrow I may not see you
As I had yesterday,
For today has come,
And today He is,
And tomorrow I shall speak of him,
Yesterday.

THE END

Has our tale no happy ending
OR
Are you just going to leave it unfinished?

ODE TO A SUMMER LOVE

I left you many times,
And many times,
I left with you a part of me.
But today,
I again left you,
Yet in a different way,
I left you taking with me,
The many parts I so foolishly left behind.

TO A POEM

What can be said when there's no one left to talk to?
So I converse with my paper and make love with you.

MR. SNOWFLAKE

Softly, gently,
He brushed my face,
Passing over my hair,
Caressing my cheek,
Lingering on my lips.
I felt a chill sweep through me,
And I longed to return his touch.
I slowly brought my hand to my face,
And opened my eyes.
He was gone.
My lips were wet.

LOVE DEFINED

Love is one saying "I know" in response to a glance.

A TOAST

And here's a toast to all my friends.
I have no drink, just simple words,
To thank you for the confidence,
The sense of pride and worth you've given me.
For making me laugh when there've been tears on the way,
For sharing my dreams, even when they're unreal,
For helping me through when the view gets too dark,
For just being here for me when I feel alone.
Yes, here's a toast to all of my friends,
For, for,
For being just that,
All of my friends!

FOUR-LETTER WORD

Trembling,
I've heard it is.
I tremble,
And yet possess it not.

A STRANGER'S EYES

I'm looking through stranger's eyes,
And gazing at a foreign world,
All has changed,
Yet here I am still searching.

I'm looking through stranger's eyes,
And meeting unfamiliar smiles,
Wondering, ever wondering,
If one stranger's eyes I'll meet,
And together we'll find we're really not strangers at all.

ACTING

Why is my stand-in always needed when I come center stage?

TOKEN OF LOVE

I'll write you a poem,
So you can read
Words written on my heart;
I'll compose you a tune,
So you can sing
My thoughts when we're apart.
I'll recite you a verse,
So you may hear
Words I cannot, myself, express,
And if none of the afore-mentioned methods work,
I guess I'll just have to break down and call you!

DREAMS

Why must my Love be Dreams?
Is it that my Dreams prevent Love?

MANKIND REVISITED

Man was visited,
Yesterday,
By Animal
So I heard,
And Man chose to use Him selfishly,
As Man is apt to do;
Yes, Man may speak
Of words polite
And Man may intellect be,
Yet notice the Kind follows Man,
Ha! The joke is on he.

TO TOUCH

I think it's just the wind touching the night leaves
To remind us that to touch is to be.

ODE TO RAIN

A thrashing sound
You make,
As your appearance
Shatters all sunny thoughts.
Yet, you seem to bring a bond of joy,
Of feeling content,
For being inside and not being caught in your spell.

COMMIT THYSELF

Commit thyself and turn not back
Is my advice to thee,
For indecision will vex thy mind
And only a nuisance be.

THE COMMENCEMENT

A commencement, how funny;

A beginning, I thought it an end.

Yet here I stand, not at a roadblock,

But at crossroads, crossroads spelling LIFE and disappearing in
the wood.

I may travel the road of Frost, less travelled by,

Making all the difference, but should I?

Or better yet, do I want to?

Here I stand,

Act I of "LIFE" at a close.

Still the play moves on

And so must I,

Though I haven't a script,

No role or lines rehearsed,

Only a name and a face

And a piece of paper that reads "High School Graduate."

Wow, I'm confused, even a bit sad

That I have lost the security

Of a role in Act I,

A role I played every day,

Every day for four consecutive years!

But life is a continuum of yesterdays, todays and tomorrows,

None of which can be isolated.

So, this is not an end, just a mere transition,

A rest period, a time to get hold;

I'm free now!

I can be and do what I want now!

Gee, I never thought of it that way before.

A commencement.

I like that!

A beginning, not an end,

And that makes all the difference!

GOODBYE

You called and I responded to the mellow notes of autumn,
Never fearing you would be calling to merely say Goodbye.

DEATH OF A CHILD

Two days ago, a child died
In the morn when all was still.
Her death was quick, unlike her life,
Since she had wallowed in the asylum of her mind.

Two days ago, a child died,
One who lived her life in dreams,
One who dreamed her thoughts were real,
Thinking her dreams could be.

Two days ago, a child died,
One who yearned to live for love,
Yet love, ironically, was her end,
For love, she is no more.

Yes, two days ago, a child died
And, yesterday, a woman was born.

FOOLISH

How foolish one could be!
I know I was for believing anything short of "I Love You" was
    worthless.
Actually, what was said was honest and best,
And I'm sorry I didn't realize it at the time.

I SPOKE TO A FRIEND

I spoke to a friend today,
And she spoke of the man she loves,
Using such words as
Kind,
Understanding,
Loving,
Considerate,
Sensitive,
Honest,
And Gentle.
I asked her if she knew you.

SPINNING

Spinning,
No release today.
Just one step more and
Yesterday.

ODE TO MY MOTHER

There are times, blue times,
When all seems to crumble before one's eyes;
When no one seems to have a kind word or
A sympathetic ear or an open heart;
No one but one;
Thank you, Mom.

ECHO

Thunderous echo of yesteryear re-enters my Today.
Tomorrow I may not hear you as I look to the sky.
I'll feel the warmth of the sun but shivering, I'll walk inside.

AND TIME

Gazing at the smear of yellow-gold,
The moistness on my cheek
Envelops the sweet cool air of time.

Lonely as I sit,
I beckon to No One,
For they have beckoned before;
When the smear was red,
And the cheek was still dry,
And the air was warm,
And time....

Yes, and time.

TO SHARE

I found the tears displayed as if to say
They were lonely and wanting to share in the experience.

A DAY IN AUGUST

It's funny,
But my mind has wandered since I saw you,
With your long brown hair flowing,
And I questioned if our meeting was a dream.
I've thought perhaps it wasn't I you saw
But merely a girl, seemingly lonely,
Yet with friends unlike the way she spun her mind.
With change of plans,
I thought of seeking out the place we met,
In hopes of continuing our Double Solitaire,
But, NO resounded again and again,
For if you were seeking another girl seemingly lonely,
I'd rather leave our game unfinished than play alone.

TO REMEMBER

What can I say now that it's too late to say anything?
I can't say I tried, because I didn't.
I won't forget; I haven't,
But you, you might forget,

Did you ever remember?

AN OPEN LETTER

Tomorrow I would have seen you,
In the morn upon the steps
To where we spent our time learning,
Where we spoke of adolescents
And sometimes that of which we were;

Tomorrow I would have seen you,
And for hours sat complaining
With our artwork ever growing,
Though each moment was so cherished
As I sat and called the time;

Yes, tomorrow I would have seen you, but I won't,
For the time has come to call a session's end.
Yet I've contemplated returning to our steps upon the morn
To only find the shadow of two figures passing time.

Oh, but the time we passed was good,
Even when I reddened at the staring and communicating hands;
I wanted so for time to slow.
But Thursday came with sadness, as our leader made us leave.

I couldn't even say what I had planned,
Or that I really enjoyed meeting you,
Or even just good-bye;
Instead, we parted friends with a third, a friend of yours.

You told us both to "have a nice weekend".
I wanted to follow you and say my last good-bye,
But pride walked me out and gone.

Tomorrow I would have seen you, but I won't.

PLAY ON SHAKESPEARE

Am I Caesar and he, Rome?

A REALIZATION

Coming back to find autumn came and went in your absence.
Yet, sameness reaches out
Across the solitude of the white-washed house
That stood and watched the tears float by.
You were gone, searching new horizons,
To find the newness like tomorrows,
Unattainable.
Things have stayed the same, changing,
I'm sorry to say,
Whether you came and stayed or went.

POETRY EXITING

I no longer need the sound of rhyming words to make me happy.
That which filled the rhyme has been found.

ODE TO JAMES

How was I to know that the chancing of a party
Would somehow stay a marking
Of a scene to be remembered;

How was I to know that the wine and cheese and laughter
Would echo through the walls
Of a printed card reflecting;

How was I to know that the questions causing tears
Would remain a long time after
Thereby causing words so longed for to be spoken?

And yet the laughter and the tears
Have mingled with the wine
And stirred a potent drink of love
To be shared throughout all time.

www.ingramcontent.com/pod-product-compliance
Lightning Source LLC
Chambersburg PA
CBHW022025090426

42739CB00006BA/295